I0182082

True Confessions of a Real Life B.A.P.

Bisexual African-American Poet

A collection of erotic poetry and short stories from the secret life of a down-low WOMAN.

By
Adisa Salim

Parental Warning: This book is not for the weak, the faint at heart. Some of the content of my poetry may not be suitable for all audiences. So if you have a delicate disposition, stop reading RIGHT NOW!!!!!!

Dedication

Dedicated to my Jennifer, you will always be my love, my friend, and my muse.

Acknowledgements

I would like to thank my mom, Maebell Stanford, for not judging me. My children Tajee, Jasper, DeAngelo, Deonta and Darice, I love you guys. My nieces, Ayala and Tationna for loving me unconditionally. My brother, Jessie, for always being there.   Special thanks to my LGBT community, you all are the most loving, loyal, supportive group in the world. Thanks to all, much love.

Table of Content

Preface

Chapter 1 I'm coming out

Chapter 2 Spoken Word Confessionals

Chapter 3 Switch Hitter

Chapter 4 Open Marriages Rock

Chapter 5 Three's Company

Chapter 6 The Conversion

Chapter 7 The making of a cougar

Chapter 8 Still love me some him

Chapter 9 My life as a poem

Chapter 10 Miscellaneous Poems

Dictionary

Preface

In recent years, there has been much fanfare about men who are living on the down low. Down low brothas have been the subject of movies, TV shows, music videos, news articles, and bestselling books. For those of you who do not know what "down-low brotha" means, it is a term used to describe African-American men who live a heterosexual life to the outside world but are underground homosexuals. In the age of AIDS, a down-low brotha is viewed as the lowest form of life. He has sex with men and women and doesn't reveal his true sexuality to either partner. We hear so much about the down-low man but what about the down-low woman?

I was hard pressed to find anything on the internet about down-low sistas because I knew they exist. You see, I lived my life on the down-low for almost 20 years. I hid behind my marriage and my children. I appeared "normal" to everyone around me. No one ever suspected. No one questioned. I was a straight, "happily" married woman.

Just like men, you cannot point out a "DL sista", but trust me they are everywhere. You can't tell by their jobs or by the way they look; because DL sistas blend in perfectly with society, just as their male counterparts do. And even though there is a double standard when it comes to DL women, there is still that fear. The fear of being judged, fear of prejudice, fear of non-acceptance, and fear of rejection keep most women in the closet.

I have heard people talk about whether homosexuality is something that we are born into or if it's a

lifestyle choice. I believe it is there from birth and we have the choice to act upon it or not. I don't believe someone can be "turned out" or "made" gay.nor do I believe a gay person can go straight. I tell people, I would still be bisexual even if I **never** had sex with a woman. I cannot change my sexual orientation. The same principle would apply to a straight person. If a straight person never had, or stop having sex, they would still be straight.

Who in their right mind would choose this lifestyle?

Who would risk being the victim of hate crimes?

Who would want to be ostracized by their friends and family? I have noticed that a lot of my DL sistas embrace the fact that they are single. They declare their independence. They don't need a man. But the truth is **THEY DON'T WANT A MAN.** I have heard these women say that a man can't do anything for them but pay a bill, take out the trash, or something like that. I laugh now when I see profiles on social websites of women that I know are on the down-low. They will write on their profile that they are only interested in men. I ain't mad at them because not too long ago I was one of those women.

Chapter 1

I'm coming out

It wasn't until Thanksgiving 2008 that I came out to my family, I was 36 years old at the time. It was never my intentions to allow anyone, let alone my family, to know what I had done for so many years in secret. But wait, I am getting ahead of myself; let me go back to the beginning. I knew in elementary school that I was bisexual. Now that I am looking back I probably knew before then. My first concrete memory of having a crush on a girl was during the time when little boys had stop being gross disgusting creatures to girls and little girls began to see them in a different light. I was in the fifth grade and that's when I knew for certain that I was different. At about 12 years old my feelings towards boys and girls began to change. Even at that young age I knew those feeling had to be suppressed and ignored. I did what I saw all girls my age do, chase after boys! But secretly it was the girls that held my attention.   In my opinion, out of the entire non-straight population, bisexuals are the most misunderstood group. {First Rant}- (Clearing throat) Ok...Ready? People tend to look at bisexuals as confused individuals and often call us greedy. Why? Because there is a belief in both the straight and gay community that bisexuals cannot make up their minds which sex they want to be with. Being bisexual is no more of a choice than being homosexual. A homosexual did not choose to be born that way and neither does a bisexual. I am not confused. I know exactly who I like: both men and women! Why does it bother lesbians so much that I am attracted to men? I have had lesbian women tell me that they don't date "dick dykes". (I just love that term) I know plenty of lesbians that dress in men clothes, cut their hair off to look more masculine, walk, talk, and live their lives like a man but they don't understand my attraction to men? What the hell? Are you serious? If men aren't attractive, then why the hell are all these studs trying to be one? (I've included a dictionary for those that don't know gay terminology).

I am a woman that is attracted to other women. Women! I want my woman to look like a woman, act like a woman, smell like a woman, dress like a woman, and carry herself like a woman. When I want a man, I want a real man not a pseudo-man. Why is that so hard for people to understand? Sorry Studs, I know what I just said will piss some of ya'll off, but ya'll know you're wrong with that dick dyke shit. I don't judge people. Live and let live is my motto. We are who we are and we fall for who we fall for, so let's stop putting labels on folks and just live. Who knows, I may meet a stud that will completely change my feelings towards dating one. (Hope so, fingers crossed.)   {End Rant}- breathing, breathing...Ok, now back to my story. I have also heard the myth that bisexuals will never settle with one sex because they will always be thinking about the other sex. The truth is bisexuals can be as monogamous as anyone. Just because I am attracted to both doesn't mean I have to have both. Ok, let me explain it in heterosexual terms. If you are a straight man, you are attracted to women, right? Now suppose you get married to a woman, will you stop being attracted to other women? Of course not, you got married, you didn't go blind. Now if it is in you to cheat then that attraction will lead to more. But if you are a faithful person, it will remain just that...an attraction. Being faithful is an individual decision and has nothing to do with sexual orientation. Ok, I'm off my soap box and back to my story of coming out. When I was a teenager, I married a man and even though at this point I had never been with a woman, I still knew that I was bisexual. Once I married, I thought those feelings would simply go away. I was wrong. I was probably around 19 years old when a chance encounter with a woman confirmed what I already knew, I loved women. My husband's cousin had started visiting me on a regular basis. She and I would sit on the couch, watch TV and just talk. One day out of the blue she asked me if I had ever thought about kissing a girl. Panic set in. Could she look at me and tell I had those desires? Why would she ask me that? What do I say? My mind was racing so I did what I had always done…Deny, Deny, Deny, everything. HELL NO! WHY THE FUCK WOULD I EVER THINK ABOUT KISSING A GIRL? THAT IS GROSS! AND GAY! AND WRONG! Side note: anyone that acts like this when they are questioned about their sexuality; I am willing to bet a dollar to a bucket of shit, they're gay, or at least leaning really hard that way. I think my denial just fueled the fire, because she went from questioning to pushing the issue about trying it. We are sitting on the couch and she asks if she can kiss me and this time I say yes. I think

I did it more out of exhaustion; I was tired of fighting, tired of running, if it was a part of me, then I was just going to face it once and for all. I planned to confront those desires and then bury them. The first time that I kissed a girl was just like in the movies with all the bells, whistles and fireworks. I knew after that first kiss that I was in trouble! We were both married at the time but for me, I knew there was no turning back. She and I went on to have a three-year relationship. I believe my husband felt that I was cheating because he took steps to try and catch me cheating but he couldn't. He would pretend to go to work and come home to watch the house, waiting on a man to show up at my door and it never happened. He checked phone records to see if a strange man was calling and he never found anything. He was always looking for a man, but there was never a Man. I probably could have gotten away with cheating forever but my damn conscience got in the way. Every day the guilt of cheating kept growing and growing until I couldn't take it anymore. I just couldn't take living a lie. As strange as it may sound after living this way for 3 years, I couldn't take the sneaking anymore. I couldn't take the cheating. I confessed. Guess how my husband reacted? Nope, he wasn't angry. Try again. Nope! He wasn't hurt. He was embarrassed. I suppose that made him feel like less than a man because I wanted to be with a woman. He poured on the guilt. He told me my family would disown me, my kids would hate me; people would try to hurt me if they ever found out. WOW! What could I say to that? Nothing! I just made the choice to never be with a woman again. And I kept that promise for many, many years until we divorced. My divorce was at the beginning of my journey into the "new" me. All I had ever known was being a wife and a mother so when I became single after almost 20 years I immediately jumped back into another relationship. Since I had spent so much of my life living a lie and not being true to myself, I didn't want to start my new relationship off the same way. I made up my mind that I would be honest with my new man from the beginning. Let's call the new man, Mark. Before Mark and I became too deeply involved I sat him down for the "talk". I told him that I was bisexual and that I had been in relationships with women in the past and I was still very much attracted to women. Mark said that he was cool with it and it wouldn't bother him if I wanted to have a girlfriend on the side. Say what? I thought he was joking but he insisted that he did not have a problem with me and other women. I thought that this must be my lucky day. Well, that lasted until the day that I met Jennifer. Jennifer and I met when I went to a football game with some friends. Since she lived in the area, my friends decided to stop by and visit her (for a minute). There was an immediate attraction from the first moment that we met. Thinking this was just going to be a onetime meeting, I didn't really say much to her. A few weeks later my friends threw a party at their house and as I was waiting there for other guest to arrive, guess who walks in? Jennifer! She was prettier than the first time I met her and I knew this time it was going to be more than casual conversation. Every chance I got I made an excuse to touch her, to sit close to her. She noticed that her legs needed some lotion, so I pulled a bottle out of my purse, got down on my knees and rubbed lotion on her legs. I was pretty sure I had her at that point. We shared our first kiss that night. I had fallen for her in a big way. Excited I came home to share the news with Mark. I did not receive the response that I hoped for. He was not happy at all. I let him talk to Jennifer and meet her, thinking that once he met her, he would fall in love with her the way I did; big mistake. Matters went from bad to worse. He became very insecure and jealous. He told me that I was not allowed to see or talk to Jennifer ever again. He gave me an ultimatum; it was him or her. So, I chose her. Mark was furious. The threats started at this point. "If you leave, I will out you to your family and friends". I couldn't believe that he was threatening me but I believed his threats. So much so that I didn't leave; I stayed and tried to make the relationship work. But how do you live with someone that is basically blackmailing you? I just couldn't take it anymore so I moved into the guest room. I told him we would just be roommates and split all bills until I could move into my own place. He agreed at first but our agreement didn't last long. Mark sent me a text message and told me if I continued to live in his house that I was going to continue to give him sex every day and head a few times a week. Seriously? Oh, hell naw. That was the straw that broke the camel's back. I went to my mom first and told her that I was bisexual and I was in love with a woman. My mother's response was simply ok. She proceeded to call my auntie though and tell her, "You know your niece is gay." Gotta love my mama. Next, I told my kids. They were so nonchalant about it that I thought they didn't understand what I was saying. I kept repeating that I had a girlfriend and I was bisexual, until my son said, "Mama, we get it you like girls. Can we go now?" And just like that I came out.

Chapter 2

Spoken Word

Confessionals

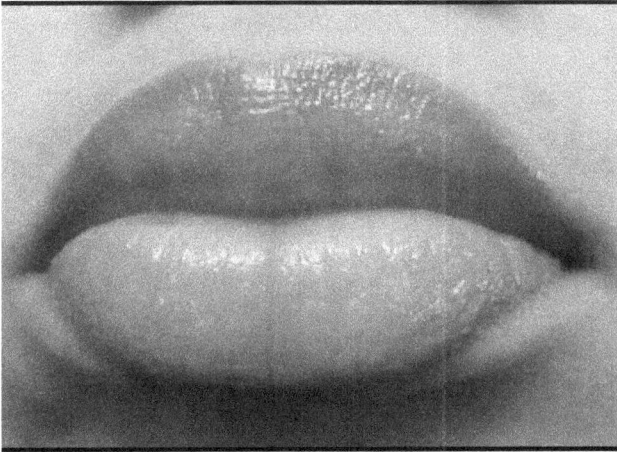

Before I came out I always expressed myself through my writings. I was free to be myself when I wrote. Often times I would write about my affairs with women disguising it under the illusion that I was talking about a man. Sometimes I felt the need to admit it. I liked women. When I would write about it though, those writings were often destroyed and never shared. The way I came out to the world was through my poetry, Spoken Word. Spoken Word is the verbal expression of poetry that really became popular after HBO started Def Poetry Jam. Well, I was at a poetry event and marveled at the way poets got on the mic and expressed themselves so freely. They talked about subjects that were controversial and sometimes taboo. If the crowd was feeling them they would clap or snap their fingers in acceptance. That's exactly what I wanted, I wanted acceptance. I went home and wrote my first spoken word piece. I titled it, My First Lesbian Experience. I thought that if I am going to do this, I am going to REALLY do this. No half stepping, I wasn't going to worry about being politically correct. I wasn't going to worry about being liked. I was just going to be me. The next month I went back to the club that hosted the open mic. I told my friend that I had written a piece and to put me on the list for open mic. I waited for my turn and when it came, I walked up to the mic...and froze. I looked into the first few rows and it was filled with elderly people. I had written a racy, very sexual piece on lesbianism and was about to say it in front of people that looked like my grandparents. Hell to the naw! I was frozen. I couldn't speak. I couldn't move. I couldn't walk back to my seat. I closed my eyes and began to speak.

MY FIRST LESBIAN EXPERIENCE

I have concealed

these feelings for so long

hiding behind societies ideals,

thinking it was wrong

but never losing the appeal

of what it would feel

like to kiss another female

and now that I have...the feeling is surreal

Like a dream

it seems that our lips were perfectly matched

I had to snatch away to catch

my breath scratching my head

as you lead me to bed

dazed, I'm amazed that after one kiss I'm attached

You have become the teacher

and even though I am your eager student

I'm still acting prudent

I am ready for our lovemaking to begin

but I'm afraid to give in

and let go because isn't loving another woman supposed to be

a sin?

I can't win

this internal battle of morals

keeps raging within.

If it is wrong why does it feel so natural?

I can't bring myself to touch you

and I don't want to seem rude

or have you think that I'm not in the mood

but I am standing before you fully clothed

and I still feel nude

not knowing what to do

Exposing the most intimate part of my soul to you

You walk toward me and push my back against the door

I close my eyes and you kiss me some more

I can't ignore the throbbing and the wetness pouring from my

very core

I have never felt so adored

with such passion like this before

I lean against the door closing my eyes tightly

And you don't rush as you slightly

touch every inch of my body

Your kisses feel like butterflies

landing so lightly all over me

I'm a ship lost at sea

 a closed lock and you are my key

I need you now to complete me

As you lead me to the bed I have come to some degree

of acceptance

This is who I am, this is me

and like opening a cage door

your love making will set me free

Men take for granted and have become impervious to the

female shape

But to me the body of a woman is the most beautiful object

God could create

And as we lie in bed

our body's wrapped around each other

I feel it is my fate

Could I have found my soul mate?

Yes baby, I think I have; I must admit it

as I felt your tongue flick across my clit

and it felt so good I wanted to say quit it

had me going insane like I should have been committed

when I felt your fingertip slip pass my lips

and dip into me

I climaxed almost instantly,

body shaking like I had Parkinson's disease, please

don't make me wait I was begging to taste you now

wow,

is all I could say when you placed

your pussy in my face

and allowed me to have a taste

and I came again just from tasting you

Making me climax multiple times

before climbing on top of me and grinding

your pussy into mine until I felt completely drained

and I can't explain

how I've sustained

life without you when you are now the blood in my veins

the beat of my heart

and as you lie on top of me and start

to drift off to sleep

I realize that our hearts have become one beat

I finally feel complete and I repeat

to myself what I've known all along

that nothing this beautiful, this natural could ever be wrong

I did it! I couldn't even look at the audience. I lowered my head and walked back to my seat in silence. Complete Silence!!! I mean you could hear crickets chirping when I was done. My heart dropped. I already started to plan out where I would move and what name I would pick when I changed names. Then, just like in the movies, a slow clap started. Before I made it back to my seat, those few claps had turned into thunderous applaud. I had my Sally Fields moment, "You like me, you really like me." And with that one poem, I started my journey to complete freedom. It was both liberating and intoxicating. I knew in that moment that the closet door I hid behind all those years was opened. and I would never go back in the closet again. I was free. I was ME.

My Dream

You are making my job today extremely difficult to do

Cause instead of getting any of my work done I'm thinking

about you

I'm writing on pink sticky notes my first name in various

combinations with your last

Afraid that this new love, will turn out like the old, you know,

same script, different cast

Or maybe this is just some phase that will pass…God I hope

not

Because you have brought out such an awakening in me that

it has caught me

off guard and I am wildly and passionately

into this sexy swagger you've got

and I fought these feeling off of being in love for so long I

almost forgot

what it feels like but I've got to stop running now, I want to be

caught

I want that puppy love feel, that type of love that feels like it

will kill me if I am away from you too long

That love that makes me smile and reminds me of you every time I hear "our" song

And just like kids we are both falling asleep but neither of us wants to be the first to hang up the phone.

Are you sleepy? No. Are you sleepy? No

We both lie, and try to stay awake just a little longer

So we lie there in our beds, phone pressed to our ears listening to each other breathe

Delaying dreamland because right now what you or I may have to say is more important than sleep and even when I give in and can't fight off sleep, in my dreams are where we meet

You and I on white sand beaches

or living in a fairytale castle where I'm your Queen

And everything we ever wanted or needed was always right there

You are my dream today

that saved me from past men that had been my nightmare

but even my dreams of you cannot compare to the reality of your gentle touch and how you cater to me in a such a way that the pleasure is

almost too much to bear…ALMOST

When you kiss me right there, right there, right there

Until my legs start to quiver, the tingling from head to toe

makes my body shiver

Not from the cold, but from how boldly you demand that my

body is yours

How you stroke me, kiss me, pleasure me into submission

I don't have the strength to fight these feelings anymore,

despite how hard I've tried

tonight I have given my heart permission

To love you freely, no matter what society says about how

things should be

 our love knows no boundaries and everything is not as it

seems

So I will love you openly, now, not just in my dreams

My lover, my friend, my world, my WOMAN

You look like you can fuck

Baby, you just look like you can fuck,

like you could hit the g-spot that women need to get a nut

the place most men think is impossible to touch

you look like you could do it

like you would take me down through it

make me sweat out my perm

have my body yearning

for you like an addict craving a fix

you just look like you know how to lick chicks and do tricks

that would inflict immense amounts of pleasure, oh

whatever it is you should bottle that though

I don't know what to call your mixture of swagger and mojo

you flow

when you walk like you're walking to music, your confidence

exudes this

You have an aura of sex,

perplexed women line up to be your next

you're the object of many fantasies the subject of many

dreams

it seems that you could make women go to extremes

 make straight women want to play on the lesbian team

 you just look like you can fuck and with any luck if it's not too

much

to ask sexy can you show me what I want to see

 make me call you mamá

 put my guess to rest and let my curiosity off the hook.

 Do you fuck as good as you look?

Chapter 3

Switch Hitter

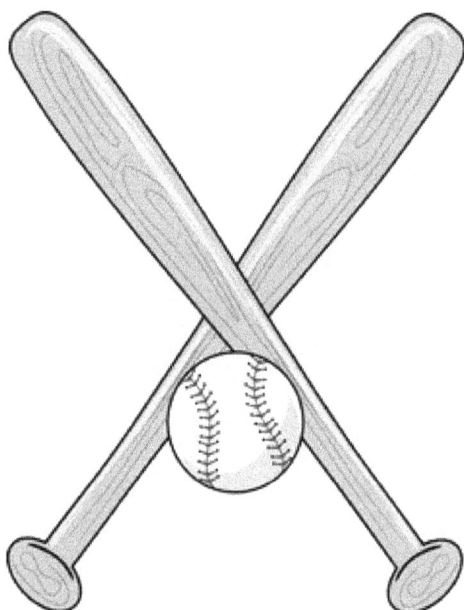

I had just come out of the closet to my family and my community. I often proclaimed myself to be lesbian, but that was not true. It took me a minute to realize that I was still not being true to myself. My lesbian friends kept telling me to choose a team. I had one friend tell me that saying I was bisexual was just a cop out. She accused me of saying I was bisexual because it was more acceptable and it would give men a false hope that I could be converted back. I am going to discuss that whole "conversion" thing later. So to make things right with the gay community that I was now officially a card carrying member of, I said that I was lesbian. Yea right, I was a lesbian that still wanted and needed a man. It is not as black and white as people think it is. Homosexuality and Heterosexuality are just two colors in the broad spectrum of sexuality. There are many other colors along that rainbow. I had lived my life being limited and defined by society's standards. I had been pressured to fit into what was perceived to be a "normal" life. I broke free but found myself still under that same pressure to conform to what the gay community considered "normal". If I wasn't gay, then I was straight. If I wasn't straight, then I was gay. Don't straddle the fence. Look, I am no fence straddle. I am BISEXUAL, in every sense of the word. I am attracted to both. I love both. I enjoy sex with both (occasionally at the same time). There is just something about the softness of a woman. The way she smells. The way she taste. The way she feels. I am attracted to every aspect of a woman. I notice their walk, their voice, their lips and eyes. I love women because they are not men. I love the fact that they are opposite which is why I personally have never dated a stud. I love the strength

of a man. I love the roughness. I am generally
very submissive to my man and very dominate
with my woman.

Because I am Bi

People don't understand bisexuality, they say
it can't be
No one can love both men and women both
equally
But I would have to disagree
Because I love them both
They say I just want my cake and eat it too
I say they don't have a clue
Saying I am a freak incapable of love is
untrue
Because I love deeply
Straight people don't know what bisexuals go
through
Dealing with the stigma of doing something
taboo
I am not her to make your fantasies come true
Because I am more than that

And my love is not confined to the feelings
between my thighs

Or simply what is pleasing to my eyes

I fall in love with the person whether it's a
girl or a guy

Because I love a person's heart

I love the gentleness of a woman, her style,
her grace

I love the softness of her lips and her
delicate face

I love the way she feels, the ways she smells
the way she taste

I love the sensuality of a woman's embrace

Because I love women

I love the strength, the swagger and the
masculinity that men possess but when he
cries I don't love him any less and I can't
forget about all the times he pulls me to his
chest and loves me until he has relieved all
my stress

Because I love men

Being bisexual is not a cop out or a plea it's

just one color on a broad spectrum of

sexuality and maybe if you could open your

eyes to see you could learn to love a bisexual

woman just like me

Chapter 4

Open Marriages

Rock!

I love the thought of an open marriage. According to Wikipedia, "an open marriage typically refers to a marriage in which the partners agree that each may engage in extramarital sexual relationships, without this being regarded as infidelity." I know the thought of an open marriage freaks a lot of women out while at the same time it makes a lot of men stand up and cheer. Ok, I know all the bible verses about marriage and homosexuality. I've heard that God made Adam and Eve and not Adam and Steve. I know that a lot of people view the sanctity of marriage as only being between two people. I know all of this. But…Ok, just hear me out for a minute. Clear your mind. Several prominent men in the Old Testament were polygamists. Abraham, Jacob, David, Solomon, and others all had multiple wives. In 2 Samuel 12:8, God, speaking through the prophet Nathan, said that if David's WIVES AND CONCUBINES were not enough, He would have given David even more. Solomon had 700 wives and 300 concubines. We are basically animals. Sex is an essential need. It is as basic of a need as food, water, and shelter. What is the purpose of sex? It is to procreate, to make babies.

How can a man improve his odds of reproducing? The more women he has sex is the greater his chance that he will produce an offspring. The need to reproduce is a driving force for humans just like animals. Think about nature, have you ever seen one lion with one lioness. NOOOOOOOOOO!! He has a whole pride, because the more females in his pride the more likely he is to reproduce. It is the survival of his species that drives him. Humans have that same driving force.

During my marriage my ex-husband cheated often. I knew he cheated, hell, I expected him to cheat. I would often try to get him to confess to his infidelities so that we could have an open conversation about what was going on in our marriage. But he would always deny cheating. I would try to simplify things for him by telling him that if he cheated to just make sure he used a condom. Again, he would deny cheating. I explained that we had been married for so long that if he craved some variety I could understand that. He still denied cheating. I explained that if I loved steak but ate a steak dinner every night for 20 years I would get tired of steak. I would want to have some chicken, fish, even a burger sometimes. Craving variety is not wrong. But of course, he continued to lie.

I still don't understand his need to lie. I wasn't angry about his affairs. I had always cheated on him with women. I was cheating with women and he was cheating with women so why cheat? We should have just had an open marriage. People often asked, if I was so nonchalant about the infidelity then why did I get divorced? His last affair was with a woman that was rumored to be on drugs. I spoke with her over the phone and she told me she had been sleeping with my husband and they had never used a condom. I never told my husband not to cheat but if he cheated to use a condom. The cheating I could deal with, him putting my life at risk I couldn't. The funniest thing about his last affair was the fact that she thought she was the only mistress. Baby Girl, was clueless. I divorced him, then He married the girl he had cheated on me with. I did sleep with him a few times after he married his current wife just out of spite. I just wanted to see what it was like to fuck someone else's husband. Truth be told, it was someone of the best sex we had. I would much rather have been his mistresses than his wife. But the difference between her and I is that I always made him wear a condom.

I told ya'll baby girl was clueless didn't I. She still thinks she changed him and she is the only one. I tried to tell her when she moved up from mistress to wife that she left an opening on his roster for a new mistress. Honey, the game doesn't change, just the players.

Loving a Married Man

When you hung up the phone, I sang there's no future in loving a married man

If I can't see you when I want

 I'll see you when I can

Damn!

Man, how many times have I heard the lyrics to that song?

Yet the first time we got a chance to be together alone

even though I knew it was wrong,

I trusted you which is not something I am prone to do

but I couldn't help how I felt

like a moth to the flame I was drawn to you.

It's a never ending cycle, when will it end

I know that it is wrong but I keep doing it all over again

My friends tell me there's no future in loving a married man

I tell them to shut the fuck up, I got u boo We already have a plan

In just a short while, I am going to marry you

You promised to love, honor and take care of me too

And you are a good man, a good man, so I know what you'll do

Fast forward to a few years later…

Every time the phone rings I get that sinking feeling in my stomach

Makes me so nauseated feel like I have to vomit

Cause I remember how you stored my name under "Joe"

pretending I was some guy calling so your wife wouldn't know

At the time I thought she was stupid and laughed at what we did

I was your little secret but now I wonder what other secrets you have hid

Man I thought that I would just move into her house and take over her life

But all I've known is strife since I went from being your mistress to your wife

You pampered me when I was just your girl showering me with gifts and promising me the stars

but I didn't know your wife earned all the money and had paid for your house and cars

And in the divorce she would get to keep every bit of it

and I would get nothing man this is some bullshit.

since she made you take all the kids she could have thrown us a freaking bone wish I had known I would be in a trailer with her kids and she would be in a nice home all alone

I thought the court would at least order her to pay some child support or something

 but no since you were the one caught cheating you walked away with nothing

I remember laughing about the double life you led

and plotting to steal you from her as you slept in my bed

But I didn't have to try to steal you she gave you away for free

cause see she knew something that I didn't know. Your ass is SORRY

Oh my god, why won't you go out and find a damn job

 instead of sitting around the house doing nothing you fucking lazy slob

I am sick of coming home from work and you're playing games on Wii

You haven't cleaned or cooked and your kids are fucking hungry

Now I am not a lesbian everyone knows that is a fact

but if I could I would marry your ex-wife and give your sorry ass back

You make me want to commit murder or suicide by slitting my wrist

I have had my fill of it, I can't take no more of this shit

The moral of the story...

Be careful what you ask for because you just might get it

Why I don't write about love

People ask me all the time, "Why don't you write about love?"

Honestly, I don't write about it because I don't know what it is

I know the attachment of love, the bonding, I understand the concept,

But even after 20 years of marriage I don't think I've been in love yet

And for real most of the time when people talk about love

It's just the make believe fairytale stuff that movies are made of

What is falling in love? Please, can anyone answer me?

I looked for answers in the bible starting with the first couple, Adam and Eve

I went back and read the entire book of Genesis and I found it odd

There is no mention of them loving each other, or either of them loving God

They were they only two people on earth so there was no choice as to who they dated

No mention of love, just of shame when they figured out they were naked

Why?

Because that was the beginning of sexual desire, that is where lust began

They were ashamed because they could see and understand the difference now between a woman and a man

It made them desire each other and there are no instructions for either of them on how to have sex

But there is no doubt; they somehow figured it out because children came next

I think we have all bought into this whole love misconception

If love was so important why isn't it a requirement for conception?

Does anyone else find it crazy that you don't even have to

LIKE the person you are with and can still make a baby?

All it takes is sex, That's it, what does love have to do with that

shit, be fruitful and multiply wasn't just based on luck. God

knew if he made sex feel good we would all go out and fuck

And the entire population of the world would begin to grow

I may not have all the answers but this is one thing I know

Lust is the initial passionate sexual desire that promotes mating, this is how we conceive children and it has nothing to do with who we love or even who we're dating.

Does anyone find it strange that to create a baby a man has to cum, but they can still make a baby even if the woman doesn't get one

Men want us to believe in love but it's all just some twisted plot

It's just sex that is why a man has to bust a nut and a woman does not

That further lets me know that love is not as important as sex

So if you ever guessed, God is a man, this is proof that you're correct

I've saw people who were in love go through all kinds of ups and down, lows and highs

crying and stalking, talking about killing themselves, when they need to go see a psychiatrist and get some help

Listening to Lenny Williams sing, I love you,

with tears in their eyes

Trying to theorize why the other person would lie

and cheat, why would they leave?

You're like O'marion now, there's an icebox where your heart

used to be

They said they loved you right? but last night,

you caught them with someone else and now you ready to

fight

That is just tooooo much drama for me,

 so I don't worry about love,

I would rather just fuck and be happy

THE NATURE OF THE BEAST

See baby you didn't have to cheat, I understand the nature of

the beast

but what I didn't understand was the lies and deceit

You had the best of both worlds... your wife and your girl

but you couldn't be content so now the drama's bout to unfurl.

I told you that I could understand the cheating it was the lies I

despised

You weren't just some random guy we were married, had ties

that bind

but that good guy disguise

has led to the demise of our relationship and I'm through with

this shit

so the gloves are off we bout to do this

I tried to explain cheating is not some new inventions when

you started hanging out with your boys I knew your intentions

I tried to relieve some of the tension

that was building up between us when

I called for that intervention

I sat you down and explained it like this, baby don't forget

I have been with you for 20 years

and through all our blood, sweat, and tears

I get tired of your ass too

I already knew about that stuff that you did but I couldn't throw

away 20 years and 5 kids See being your wife

I couldn't be the jealous type

getting caught up in all the hype

cause what you had with her was just sex, right?

I mean I could love steak but could I eat the same steak night

after night

for the rest of my life?

Does craving variety make me wrong?

NO! that is why I said, you didn't have to cheat

I understand the nature of the beast

Now I'm not going to pretend like it was all on you

I had secrets I was concealing too

While you were with her thinking you were getting over on me

I was peeling down lace panties and eating my girls pussy

But when I tried to be honest with you

you made me feel like I was wrong

told me I had to leave other women alone

when all along you were doing the same thing don't think I

didn't know about all your little flings

See if we had just been honest with each other neither of us

would have had to cheat

you didn't have to turn to women in the streets

we could have went out to meet

woman to bring home for us some fun

jealousy there would have been none

that is why I said you didn't have to cheat

I understand the nature of the beast

So now, I'm divorcing you

I'm through, you can try this with another bitch because I have

had enough

You didn't think I would leave well Boo, I'm calling your bluff

Oh I'm not going to fight you for our son's, they are almost

grown

so I think it's your turn to be dad and mom

But I will take house, the car, and the furniture too

Stupid motherfucker your ass won't have shit when I'm

through

Oh yeah give me the pitbull that dog is mine and I closed the

checking and saving accounts and withdrew every dime

So now move your broke ass into the trailer park with her

cause I know living your life like a savage is what your prefer

Oh and I ran into your best friend "Stan"

and now he is my new man

and he understands my need to fuck a female plus he gets

the pussy too so everything is swell...Golly Gee, Now he has

everything YOU used to have and all you have is .. NOTHING

Oh well that is what happens when you deal in lies and deceit

you didn't have to cheat

because I understood the nature of the beast.

Why do men Cheat?

I believe it is just a part of their nature

it's programmed into their DNA

And women might get mad at me for saying what I say

but GOD designed them that way.

God made sex feel good so with any luck

we would fuck and procreate.

Think about the primates

to create an offspring they would mate with multiple mates.

It is very simple for a man to reproduce, it takes one act of sex

from a man to make baby

As opposed to nine months of pregnancy that same baby

spends growing inside a lady

So hypothetically speaking during the 9 months that a woman

spends carrying around her 1 child,

A man could fuck a different woman every night and make around 280 babies now that's wild

So when God said be fruitful and multiply he was really giving instructions to Adam

Cause while Eve was pregnant, his daughters were still birthing him daughters and son's

That's how this nation was begun and just because we have evolved and are supposed to be wiser

Doesn't mean men can just turn off that genetic marker, that natural instinct for survival

Don't think women that I am excusing men for cheating, it is still wrong you see

But the cheating is not the problem; the problem is a man's lack of honesty

If he wants to go out and do what he wants to do

He should at least be man enough to come straight out and tell you

And let it be your choice if you want to stay or go

instead of putting your life at risk without even bothering to let you know

Again, women don't think I am making excuses for men's behavior and saying that it is ok

But sometimes it's our unreal expectations that causes are relationships to decay

Men don't love like we love their love is simple and plain,

They don't know how to confess with their heart it is hard for them to verbally explain

So I am going to do it for him

Baby, when I cheat on you that doesn't mean that I don't love you

Cause I do, It's just that I am flawed and I am in awe of you

I know I don't deserve a woman like you.

You are incredible to me and out of all the men in this vast universe I can't believe you chose me. That scares me.

Because I fear that one day

you might wake up and realize that you are too good for me

and just leave.

So I use sex for my own vain selfish reason, but it doesn't

mean that I don't love you.

Actually, my brother Jessie, asked me to write that part

But I feel like I should start

to give you some stats

so women you can see just where we're at

If you are a single Black woman then your ass is in trouble

And if you are a Black woman that loves Black men

That trouble just doubled

The U.S. Census says there are 87 single, available Brothas

for every 100 Sisters

So why do single women have such a hard time finding the

Right Mister?

Why do we struggle trying to find Mr. Right and end up settling

for Mr. Right Now?

It's because the US Census is full of shit and I'm about to

break the real number down

Ok they say there are 87 single available Black men

but they didn't take out the 20 Black men

That is locked up in jail and in prison

So that leaves those 100 women 67 men to compete for

But hold on a minute

We have to take away another 20 for the Black men

that only date and marry White women.

That leaves us 47 single, available Black men ready to play,

but we have to take away another 20

for the down low brothers that are bisexual or just plain gay.

That makes our odds of finding a single available Black man

100 to 27

No wonder men cheat with odds like that they are in pussy

heaven.

You would probably hit the lottery before you find a good, faithful, single Black man

You want to know why all Black men cheat. Hell, they cheat because they can.

Why do men cheat? No reason they could give would be good enough

Honestly, most men don't have a reason, they cheat just because

See, men and women, we are cut from a different cloth

Women use sex for affection and love and men use sex just to get off

So women we have to stop taking it personally what men do

It doesn't mean you are somehow flawed because a man cheated on you

Men try to satisfy us and take away some of the sting

When they give us those bullshit excuses for going out and doing their thing

Saying stuff like baby you let yourself go and you're not as fine

as you once were

Well Halle Berry is absolutely gorgeous and two husbands still

cheated on her

So no boo, that's not it

They say they were just drunk and one thing led to another

and before they knew it old girl had become their lover

Well, you're not Jamie Fox, so don't blame it on the

a a a a a a Alcohol.

Cause you were drunk as hell watching the game in the

basement but you didn't fuck Jamal

Oh hell, maybe you did, but again,

that's not it

A man will try blaming you and telling you it's because you

weren't a freak

But that's not it either and that excuse is just tired and weak

You can do it everything, oral sex, anal, 3somes, slide down a

pole and buy a sex swing

And he will still want to go out in the streets and have some

random fling

So no that's not it either

You can bare him all his children and love him beyond

measure

And he will still run to the arms of another woman for pleasure

So no that's not it either

Why do men cheat? I'm sick of hearing this over and over

again I'm not trying to defend them but I will go out on a limb

And say the #1 reason they cheat is there is always a woman

willing to cheat with him.

Chapter 5

Three's Company

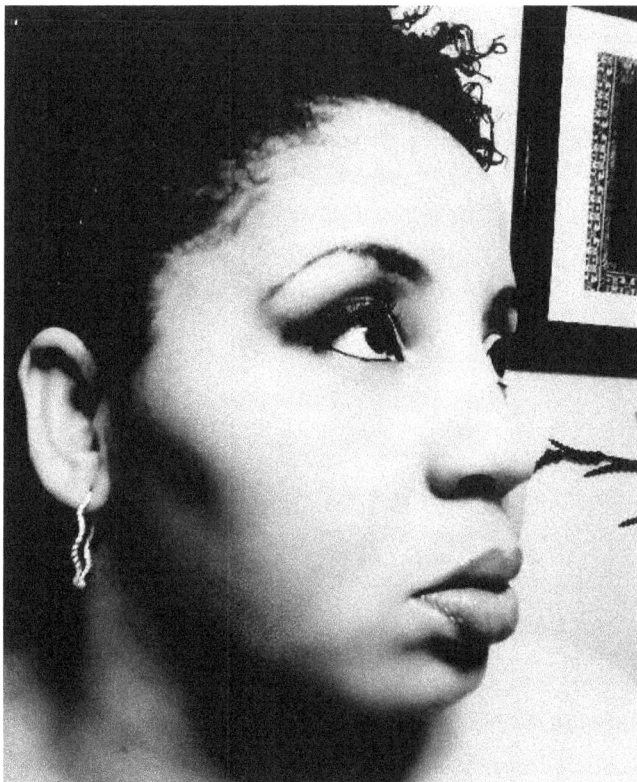

Now, there are some men that specifically seek out bisexual women. These are the men that think if they have a bisexual woman it will allow them the opportunity to have threesomes. In some cases that is the truth but not always. I have had the chance to experience sex with men and women. If you have never had a threesome I suggest you try one immediately. Now my experience with a three way love affair was positive but it did have one negative moment. Being that my girlfriend and I were both bisexual, we decided to find one man that we could include in our sex life. We started going out on dates with men. The problem was either she would like them and I wouldn't, or I would like them and she wouldn't. That was until we ran into an ex-boyfriend of hers name Rob. Rob was an attractive, very dark skinned, muscular brother that was just my type. Since she had already been with him we decided it would be easy to just include him into our relationship. At first everything worked out great. We would spend every weekend at his house. The three of us did everything together. We would go out partying together. Drink, dance, kiss, hold hands, the typical couple stuff, we did it as a trio. Everything was perfect. Until Rob and I started getting closer. See that is always a danger when you involve other people in your relationship. Rob told me that he wanted to see me alone. This would not have been a problem as long as I told my girlfriend first. He insisted that I keep it to myself and just sneak to see him on the side without her. NEGRO PLEASE!!! Did he forget that she was my girlfriend and he was basically our toy? A walking, talking, dildo was all he was. He had overstepped his boundaries and had to be put in check. My loyalty was to my woman. She was my priority and there was no way in hell I was going to let a "toy" come in between us. I told my girlfriend what happened and we mutually decided that fool had to go. Dumb ass trick! Two pussies minus two pussies leaves you with zero and that's what he got NOTHING!

Ménage' a Trio

I press her dress up raising it high, rubbing

my hand down her thigh,

and even when she whisper's a sigh

we keep our eyes locked as our bodies' rock

and sway to the imaginary music that has

invaded this space,

I almost forget we are not alone in this place

as I peel away her lace panties, I can see him

watching passion filled to the rim, he is

ready to begin

He is anxious but this is my show, I am in

control so I slow

down our urgent pace stroking gently the side

of her face

I kiss her softly on the neck while I pull her

near

so she can hear as I whisper love serenades in

her ear and I feel her legs go weak,

He cannot speak, in awe of my technique of

loving a woman

Her lips meet mine and as our tongues are

intertwined

I look at him sitting in his chair

there is so much passion in his stare

I look from her to him, from him to her and

that fire between my legs starts to stir

I am lost in the anticipation of what is about

to occur

I motion him with one finger and with catlike

quickness he is there

Standing behind me, reaching around me, his

hand in my underwear

And I feel his fingertip dip into the nectar

of my flower

and his kisses shower my body...I am helpless as

I allow them to undress me. He can no longer

prolong the agony

of delayed ecstasy as he pushes us both to our
knees

our tongues tango to taste the tip; I rub his
essence across my lips

And I give her a kiss hungrily we share his
gift, but in one swift move he grabs my hips

Now he is taking me from behind

and as he does I grind my ass back with each
thrust

until just when he is about to bust and has
reached the brink

that's when he withdraws and allows her to
drink.

As she tastes his wine, I taste hers too, who
knew that she would make my fantasy come true.

Now they are both lapping up my juice like a
kitten drinking cream

Adisa, baby it's time to get up, it was all a
fucking dream

For most men, threesomes are the ultimate fantasy. The chance to have wild, passionate sex with two women is the stuff of movies (at least the pornographic kind).

It amazes me that some of these men are so bold that they will ask me if they can fuck me AND MY GIRL. I have to laugh because most can't do shit with one woman so what the hell do they think they can do with two? Men, here's a life lesson. If you are making love to your woman and two minutes into the sex you're done…DON'T ASK ABOUT A THREESOME. Do you really think your woman wants to cut her two minutes down to one?

Ok, since this book is supposed to be an honest look into down-low women, bisexuality, and me. I am going to keep it real. Yes, I have had threesomes. (I can't believe I am going to write about this, but here goes)

When it comes to threesomes, a lot of the time closeted bisexual women will fulfill their man's fantasy to be with another woman. She will do this under the pretense that it is all about him and she is doing this just to please her man. She is just being a good woman, right?

But what her man doesn't know is that the threesome is all about her. She is doing it in order to freely have access to another woman without the stigma of being labeled as a lesbian. During my marriage, my husband never asked for a threesome. He never brought the subject up. Even when I confessed and told him that I had been cheating on him with other women, he never asked to join or even watch. My first experience with a threesome came after my marriage ended. The guy I was dating at the time brought the idea to the table. I was still very much in the closet at the time, so when he suggested it to me, I acted like I was angry. Why would I let my man screw another woman and in front of me? How could he even suggest something like this? But deep down, I wanted to. I was crazy about him and the sex was amazing; including another woman could only enhance our sex life. So I did what so many women do, I gave in. I made him think he had talked me into doing something that I didn't really want to do. I was only doing it to prove my love. Threesomes can be awesome as long as everyone involved is on the same page. Everyone has to know what they are there for and what they are going to gain from the experience. If any of the parties are jealous then what starts out as just fun can turn ugly, quickly. It's not just the women that get jealous either. Men will get jealous during a threesome if he feels like the women are more into each other than they are into him. He will feel neglected. The same holds true for the wife/girlfriend if the man is paying more attention to the other woman. It is like walking a tightrope. It is a balancing act to distribute your attention evenly. If done correctly, a threesome can be one of the most satisfying experiences of your life. I have also been in a long term three-way relationship. People don't understand this either but it is a lifestyle that I'm not opposed to trying again. Sometimes this lifestyle is confused with being a swinger but it is not the same. In my relationship we didn't swap multiple partners. I was involved in a committed relationship with a married couple. The three of us went out together, held hands, slept in the same house, in the same bed and it worked for us. I loved it.

I have had men ask me could I turn their women out because they wanted a bisexual woman.

There are occasions where I have been attracted to a straight woman.

There was a girl that I was attracted to at my church Both her uncle and father are ministers. She was very gay and very much in the closet. Once during her Sunday rant about all gay people going to hell, I text her a picture of me kissing and fingering a girl and asked her if she wanted to be next. She promptly texts me back and asked me if could she be next.

HELL YES! We dated off and on for several years.

My little Secret

You are still practically a stranger to me

I only see every once in a while, always a

pleasant smile

and sometimes a quick hug in passing

but when I am alone I find myself asking, what

is it about you,

that draws me to you like I am under some type

of voodoo

or is it some sort of witch's brew that you

have concocted that got me wanting you?

It is almost as if I have lost all rhyme and

reason and nothing is as it seems

I am not supposed to be the one with the

daydreams.

I think about you now when I am all by myself

and no matter what I try to do to tune out

those thoughts nothing seems to help

I can't shake the vision of you kissing me, so

softly; I barely feel your touch

But I want you so badly that slight kiss is

not enough

and I part your lips and give you a little

tongue, not too much

And I feel your hand cup

my breast and now you're kissing me on my neck

and I am gone

I can no longer tell where my body stops and

yours start, your moan is my moan and before

long the touch of the hand in my dreams

has become the touch of my own hand in reality

 as I bring myself to climax with thoughts of

you and me

Now when I see you, I don't see a stranger

when I look into your eyes

 but I see the ties that bind us together as

lovers

even though we have never had sex with each
other

I feel like LL in Hey Lover, whenever you're
near

Damn Girl, I ain't had a crush in years

PUSSY REHAB

I wish I was a fortune teller, or some type of
gypsy

That could look into your future and know your
history

Cause If I had known that you were going to
act like this

I would have never, ever, ever, ever given you
any pussy

And I understand you were a little unprepared
for what happened

But I told you, you weren't ready for this
when you kept asking

Telling me how you would make me call you
daddy and have me screaming

I told your ass to wake up because you were
obviously dreaming

And now your dreams have become my nightmare,
wish I had kept walking

Because I only gave you a little pussy and
you're already stalking

I can imagine how you would have acted if I
had gave you a little head

Then you probably wouldn't have stalked me but
become suicidal instead

And I am sooo glad that I didn't mess around
and give you any ass

Cause then you would have been like Kathy
Bates in misery

And kept me chained down to the bed

I wanted you to know that I have caller ID so
I know it's you when you call

That holding the phone and breathing heavy
into it doesn't turn me on at all

And I don't feel sorry for you when you tell
me all the time

How you can't eat, don't sleep and how you can't stop crying

I told you, I call my pussy the snapper but you thought it was a joke

Told you it was more addictive than crack and you weren't ready to smoke

But you had to try it for yourself and now look at you

Having withdrawals, shaking and shit, just don't know what to do

So this is an intervention, grab your shit, I'm calling you a cab

Cause you are addicted to my pussy and need to go to rehab

Fuck 12 steps as bad as you are you need 20 more

I have to show you tough love, even though I hate being hardcore

Because I know that sometimes stalkers can take things too far

And I don't want to end up in the trunk of

your damn car

So guys please stop asking can u fuck me and

telling me what you can do

I don't need any more stalkers, I have plenty

already so let's not add you

The Snapper

They call me snapper, not to be confused with
the clapper
no two claps of my hand will turn you off or
on
But I'm talking about pussy so good you'll try
to cash in all your cootchie coupons
trying to trade some of my pussy for shopping
sprees and trips to the salon
why is it called a snapping pussy, I have
heard people ask
well I am about to break it down for you at
last
The term "snapper" came from the snapping
turtles that may live in a swamp or marsh
The turtle will clamp down and not turn loose
even if you cut his head off
and I know that seems harsh

But Snapper means powerful muscles and a
genuine death- grip

And that is what my snapping pussy does when I
flip

you over and start gyrating these hips

Men, I have to warn you making love to a

snapping pussy can be a religious experience

And if you are not prepared it will catch you

off balance

A man doesn't even have to move, hell I don't

have to move either

Everything I do is done internally with very

little effort, you see

but the effects will make him cum almost

instantly

See, I know some of ya'll don't believe me

and think a snapping pussy is myth, rather

than fact

A true snapper can crack a raw pecan in her

cootchie

then spit out the shell, leaving the nut
intact.

A true snapper can take the lid off an
imported beer bottle

and never use her hands

 A true snapper can handle a raw egg without
breaking it

and then turn right around and crush a 12 oz
Coke can

So the next time you hear someone asks, what
makes pussy good

Tell them it's the muscle control, the way a
woman can squeeze your manhood

We all know that all pussy was not created
equal…but what makes a kitty purebred?

It's when a woman makes a man cum when all he
managed to get in was the head

So all you women before I leave I want you all
to rejoice

And if You HAVE A SNAPPING PUSSY LADIES, LET
ME HEAR YOU MAKE SOME NOISE (snap, snap)

SIDE NOTE: NOW THAT YOU HAVE READ THE SNAPPER,
YOU SHOULD UNDERSTAND WHY I HAD TO GO BACK AND
WRITE PUSSY REHAB. DANG MEN THEY WILL GET
STUPID OVER SOME GOOD PUSSY. I STILL LOVE THEM
THOUGH.

Chapter 6

The Conversion

There is a misconception that a person can be "turned out". This is absolutely false. NOBODY and I mean NOBODY can turn a person gay. If that person is gay it is because they already had those tendencies anyway. Now, can someone help you explore that hidden sexuality and bring it to light? Yes! But they didn't create the other person's sexual identity. I'm sure everyone has seen Tyra or Oprah do the makeover shows. They will take a plain Jane and style her hair, put her on makeup and put her in some new clothes. Surprise!!! Jane has become a knockout. She is beautiful. Did they make her beautiful? No! Oprah and Tyra didn't create her. Everything that she needed to be beautiful was already there. What they did was enhance what was already there. This is how I view the whole conversion process. A gay person did not turn a straight person gay. Their sexuality was already there.

There is a big thing now in the lesbian population where women have been so mistreated by men that they are becoming gay. WRONG! I don't care how much someone is mistreated, No one can drive you to be gay. I think this misconception is aimed more towards women. I have had men ask me who has hurt me because they assume that is the reason I like women. I usually respond by asking them if a woman ever hurt them. If the answer is yes, I ask them, "why are you not gay then?

During my marriage I would cheat more with women when things were going really bad. It was just comforting to me to be with another woman. Most women have gone through the same thing with men so we understand each other. We are nurturers by nature and a lot of times our relationships are more emotional than sexual.

During a relationship I had with a woman I began going through some stuff with my husband. He had become violent. My girlfriend would beg me to leave him but I wouldn't. I left him for a while and went to the Salvation Army shelter for domestic violence but after I left the shelter we got back together. My girlfriend eventually got tired of waiting.

You, Me and He

We have been secret lovers now for the past 2
years

No eye contact in public, no touching you when
you are near

For fear that someone will guess that we are
more than just friends

And I am out the closet openly lesbian

But you are not; you are still hanging on to
that "piece" of a man

And that piece of a life that you no longer
want to be in

Afraid to get kicked out of church

But love even if it is between the same sexes
should never be a sin

Afraid your family will not love you, so you
keep your love buried within

And you are only brave enough to express it
when we are alone

For those few hours, before "HE" calls wanting to know why you are not home

So you hurriedly get dressed and rush out the door

Back to the abuse, you cried and told me you couldn't take no more

You know that you deserve better than this

He insists he loves you and you believe him

And when you resist, he reminds you how much he loves you with his fist

Then you come to me

Eyes black, lips bloody, bruises from shoulder blade to wrist

And I put you in the tub and wash away your pain like I am John the Baptist

I try to heal the internal scars with my kiss cause ice may help with the bruises on the outside

but it will take time for the pain of the internal wounds to subside you are reaching for me wanting to make love

to push the pain aside

But not tonight I just want us to lie side by

side

My arms around you, my thighs wrapped around

your thigh

Your head is nestled in the cleavage of my

breast

As I caress your face and it's not that I

don't want you that's not the case

But right now what you need is deeper than

physical love

What's in your best interest is all that I'm

thinking of

And if he won't do it, then I will place your

needs above my needs

Until you are able to stand on your own to

feet

Until you have the courage to finally break

free

Until he is no longer a part of this trinity

Until we no longer have to live our lives in secrecy

Until you, me and he

Becomes just the two of us

I will wait for you

PATIENTLY

Deer Love

A lot of hunters think that deer are just

dummies

Because they don't

rely on their eyes or ears

they don't trust what they hear

or see and that may be

hazardous in the woods

but it makes a great love philosophy

From now on I am going to love like a deer

I'm not going to trust what I see or what I

hear

Because looks can be deceiving

and that is one of the reasons

so many women fall prey

To these pretty men, who use chocolate skin

and six pack abs to woo the ladies

I see it every day

and I just can't understand

That is why I don't date pretty boys

GIVE ME AN UGLY MAN

I want a man so ugly

that I can't even look him directly in the
face

He uses default photos cause he is too ugly to
post his pictures on Facebook and MySpace

And I'm a big girl so ya'll know food is my
best friend

But I want a man so ugly I don't even want to
go out to eat with him (now that's ugly)

Cause ugly men are better lovers and I know
some of ya'll think I'm crazy for saying all
of this

But women, trust me, an ugly man will foreplay
you into unconsciousness

Cause he knows that he is lucky to have this
one chance

So he will pull out all stops when it comes to
romance

Ladies, we need to stop looking at the

exterior beauty

Be like the deer don't trust what you see

and don't put too much stock in what you hear

Don't let these men trick you

by whispering sweet nothings in your ear

Telling you everything that you want to hear

how fine and sexy you are

Don't listen to the empty promises

of how he'll give you the moon and the stars

When he starts singing Luther or R Kelly

you start singing Jesus keep me near the cross

Cause words are a powerful weapon

that can be used to talk your panties right

off

Get you a man that stutters, has a lisp

or some other type of speech impediment

That way you don't have to worry about being

seduced when he speaks

And if he stutters bad enough

by the time he get his line out...you'll be
asleep

Yes, I've learned to love just like a deer

I don't trust what I see or what I hear

Instead of using my eyes and ears

when searching for a mate, I trust the nose on
my face

Cause just like a deer

I can smell bullshit from a mile away

Purple Rain

I wish I could find a man that was find a man
that was compatible with me

I don't mean educationally or financially, I'm
talking purely sexually

I'm so sick of looking, but I really could use
some help

Wish I could clone me so that way I could just
fuck myself

YES I AM THAT GOOD!

Right now my greatest satisfaction comes from
a vibrator, ya'll guess his name. He is purple
and water proof so I call him PURPLE RAIN.

Anyway, now that I'm getting older my friend
keep telling me to get a younger man

They say girl if anyone can keep you cumming
all night a little thug can

So I went on a search for some thug love and
maybe I went to extremes

Cause I recruited a former player from my ex-husband's little league team

Ya'll don't look at me like I'm some child molester the boy is 21 now

And he was fine abs like bam and arms like POW

This boy just looked like he could fuck

But looks can be deceiving cause 5 seconds into the sex his body starts jerking and heaving

Was it good for you baby?

I know he did not just ask me that shit, maybe I misunderstood

Because I know he doesn't think that I came when he had barely got his dick in the pussy good

Fucking premature ejaculator

So maybe that young thug lover was not meant for me

I went from a man young enough to be my son to one old enough to be my daddy

I love the style of an older man, I love their ways

He could eat the hell out of some pussy and he took his time with foreplay

But when it came down to the fucking let's just say his erectile dysfunction kind of got in our way

I know his heart was in it and he had the will but I don't think it would have helped if he popped a whole bottle of those little blue pills

Limp dick bastard

Lately it just seems I haven't had any luck

Finding a man that really knows how to fuck

I want a man that will hit that pussy so right

He will make me want to cook him a full course meal in the middle of the night

Ya'll know like Tyrese did that chick in Baby Boy, fucked her so good she got up cooked tacos and picked up all the baby toys.

Now that is some good dick

But I guess until I can find someone to take

away this pain

I'll just have to make sure I keep extra

batteries for my Purple Rain

My Jodi

I can't believe this man is lying her snoring
in my face

Sorry ass he bout to make me catch a case

I'm about to shake him and wake him up

How the hell you going to fall asleep after
you bust a nut

And why the hell you so tired like a marathon
you just finished running

When your dick had barely passed the lips
before you ass started coming

Always talking shit to me like you done did
something great

Sorry ass, wasting my time, I could have had a
V 8

That's ok that is why I always keep Jodi on
speed dial cause unlike you Jodi will make
sure the sex is worth my while

See sweetie, Jodi is my best friend, you might know him or maybe not

But when I start saying I need some me time, it's just a plot

Because what I really got is some Jodi time

And it's not that hard for you to figure out what I'm doing

You know you been messing up so this smile is from the other man I'm screwing

Did you ever wonder why I don't trip any more about you spending time with your friends?

Why I stopped caring about you lack of ends, hell I will even lend you some money to make you go away

Because that is the time that Jodi comes over to play

So men keep being selfish, getting yours and your women not getting the same

Cause later on tonight she won't even think about you when she is screaming Jodi's name

And if you just finished fucking and all of a

sudden she has to make a trip to the store

It's cause you left her hanging again and she

if running back to Jodi for some more

So ya'll better learn some dick control while

fucking say your ABC or add some numbers in

your head

Cause if you don't satisfy your woman, you

will find Jodi in your bed

Chapter 7

The making of a

Cougar

I have never been attracted to younger people, men or women. I have always dated older. But now that I am getting older I am finding myself attracted to younger. When I was married my ex-husband coached a little league football team (12-14 year olds). Stop right there, I know what you are thinking and NO, I am not a child molester. Ok, now that I got that out the way back to my story. While he was coaching, we often allowed his team to spend the night at our house. One little boy in particular always wanted to hang out with me. I thought it was cute that he had a crush on me. Once he was too old to play football, he lost contact with our family. He went on to graduate from high school and left for college. One year when he came home to visit he comes to my home looking for his old football coach. I explained that Coach no longer lived here and that we were divorced.

He asked how I was doing and how I was handling it. After we had stood in the doorway for about 10 minutes chatting I invited him in so that we could continue to talk. We talked and he brought me up-to-date on what had been going on in his life. In the middle of our talk, he kissed me, without any warning. There was none of the typical eye contact and slowly moving in for the kiss, nope, it was fast. I was stunned and didn't have time to react. I sat there quietly. He didn't say a word. It felt like hours passed before either of us said anything. "I'm sorry" he finally said. I asked him why would he do that. He went on to tell that he has always had a crush on me but expected that it would eventually go away but it never did. He knew the age difference was a problem but he was in love with me. I looked him in his eyes and knew he was serious and that he meant every word that he was saying.

Here comes the movie moment…we looked at each other and he leaned forward slowly and kissed me. This time I kissed him back. That was the beginning of a very hot affair. I loved the sex but I didn't love him. I was ashamed of our relationship and when he started pressuring me to have a "normal" relationship, I ended our affair. He didn't understand how I could have sex with him but refused to go to a movie. I just didn't want anyone to know I was sneaking around with this boy (sorry he was a man at this point), this man, that was young enough to be my son.

Cougar Town

I am newly divorced after 20 years I'm not

really looking to settle back down, I am

enjoying the fact the I am free

But all of my new found freedom comes with a

price that I didn't think of

There is no one to shake and wake up at 3 in

the morning when I want to make love

And now that I am approaching my 40's my

hormones are out of control, they are raging

And since I'm not even dating, I have a little

purple friend I keep on my night stand for

just such occasions

But there is only so much satisfaction I can

get from my little purple plastic friend

And Fellas don't let women lie to you, toys

can't compete with real men

Well, all of my girlfriends have been telling

me I need to become a cougar

I'm asking what is a cougar? Evidently it's

when an older woman gets a younger man "a cub"

to do ya

Now there are a lot of younger men out there

that try to get with me, so choices I have

plenty

But there is just something disturbing to me

about fucking a man in his twenties

That is the same age as my son, so I would

feel like I was molesting the poor child

But like I said I'm approaching 40, horny and

damn it, it has been a while

So I'm strolling through my phone trying to

see

who the lucky person would be

when I stop on the name RC

one of my son's friend that had been hitting

on me

So I give him a call, surprised that he

answered at all

considering it's 3 am

I invite him over, 5 minutes later the door
bell rings, it's him

A little anxious are we? I wanted to ask
but before I could get the words out he was
kissing me and grabbing my ass

From the minute he walked through the door he
was being aggressive but not pushy

Told me he was going to show me what younger
men could do to some pussy

As soon as he said that I was thinking who the
hell this little boy think he is

He is still a baby, young ass, he still got
breast milk behind the ears

Someone forgot to tell him, I am SickWitIt, he
must not know

I will have him looking for me in a daylight
with a flashing light begging for some mo

At least that was what I was saying until this
boy got a hold of me and then I was lost

It felt so good when his tongue hit that spot
it made my eyes cross

And when he finally entered me he erased any
and all doubt

He kept going and going like the energizer
bunny, honey, he made me tap out

He is laughing because I'm sitting up, shaking
and shit, cause he know he hit it right

My body is so sensitive at this point if he
touches me anywhere it's going to be a fight

Don't touch me, Don't touch me So he is asking
me if he can come by and see me again

I say HELL YES, you gonna make me retire my
little purple friend

So older women get a cub it's some of the best
sex that I've found

Sorry older men I'm taking up a permanent
residence in Cougar Town

AGE AINT NOTHING BUT A NUMBER

I saw you the minute you walked through the
door, had taken in every detail of you
Carmel skin, not too slim, standing about 5'8
big breast, wide hips and narrow waist
I noticed your walk, strong and confident like
the Queens of Zulu
I noticed your style, smooth, like an
alligator lightly treading water in the bayou
Thick lips, fresh braids, long lashes, and
right behind your ear a new tattoo
Yes, in that short amount of time I had
noticed that too
But I also noticed the difference in our age,
so when I came off the stage and you attempted
to engage me in conversation,
all I kept thinking is you had only passed
your teenage years by two,

So I just came straight out and told you, I am

too old for you. I can't get any blunter

but then I hear that song, Aaliyah singing the

same thing age ain't nothing but a number

So now I am starting to wonder, and I must

admit my curiosity is getting the best of me

You telling me, stop worrying, age aint

nothing but a number, maybe, we'll see

Our first kiss, I'm thinking you don't kiss

like a child, slight tongue, soft pressure and

sucking on my lower lip for a while

Damn baby, you kiss like a grown lady

And then you took complete control of me when

it came to foreplay, driving me crazy with the

way that you touched me

Ummmm I loved everything you did, and I

thought, you sure don't touch me like a kid

And when you spread my legs and put your

tongue on my clit, I had to admit that I was

like oh shit, that's how a woman would do it

And when you made me cum so many times I lost count

My last thought was this is exactly how a woman would turn me out

No wonder older women are taken on lovers that are much younger

Made me a firm believer… AGE AINT NOTHING BUT A NUMBER

Dear John

I don't love you and I'm sorry if that is not
what you want to hear
But I thought I made it clear from day one
we're
friends with benefits
And that's the policy to which we have to
adhere
no dinner's, no movies, amusement park rides,
or trips to the zoo
no meeting the families, no spending the night
at each other's crib that is just not what we
do
and you knew that coming into this, so why all
of a sudden you want to trip?
Cause your ego can't get over the fact that
all I want from you is just some occasional
dick, that's it

Do you really think that you are all that?

That good dick translates into you being

worthy of my love?

See I knew your ass was too young

stop throwing temper tantrums and just grow

the fuck up,

You are the reason for this breakup

cause you couldn't be happy with the

occasional hookup

fuck being a cougar from now on I'm just

messing around with grownups

cause dammit you knew what was up

You were the knight to my bishop

the king to my queen

and I guess all those nights of us lying in

bed talking about everything

I guess that got your heart more involved than

I thought

guess I should have just gave you some head,

some pussy, some ass and then kicked you out

and then maybe you would not have caught

these damn feeling and everything would have

been what it ought

  to be, me calling you whenever I was horny

and you coming over fucking me daily

  AND THEN LEAVING

But now you're accusing me of deceiving you,

catching you up in a web of lies and deceits,

Nigga please, you are starting to sound just

like a whining bitch to me

See, clearly you are WAY to in touch with your

feelings, I'm just saying

I wasn't playing when I said you were the best

sex I've ever had, but all this I love you

stuff is making me mad

Just because you can eat the hell out of some

pussy doesn't mean that I want to be your wife

And just because you have 9 inches of good,

hard dick doesn't mean I want to be with you

for life

And just because you make me cum so many times
that I lose count and can't keep track
And just because you spank my ass just right
when you hit it from the back
Doesn't mean that I am going to fall in love
with you, so I guess that's the end, we're
through
Wait a minute, no more sex with you?
Fuck writing this Dear John letter I'm about
to call my boo.

Chapter 8

Still love me some

him

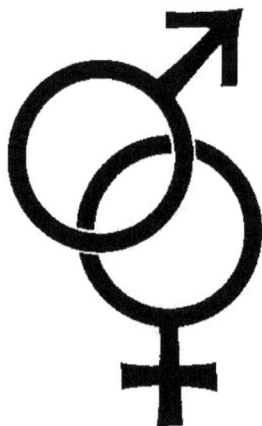

I hit on the whole "dick dyke" topic very
briefly. Lesbians especially studs don't get
why I would still have feelings towards men.
Men are beautifully strange creatures to me. I
am attracted to the way they look. I also feel
the same attraction when I look at studs but I
am not attracted to them as women but because
they have the same qualities that I find
attractive in a man. I usually don't feel the
romantic love for women that I feel towards
men. Sex with men confuses me sometimes. I
remember the first man that I was with after
me and my husband split. He was my teacher.
Even though my husband and I had a lot of sex
it was boring and routine. It took a man that
was almost 15 years my senior to really show
me the art of making love. I experienced a lot
of firsts with him. I was so confused about
what I was feeling that I thought I was in
love and even declared my love to him. Being

the older, wiser man, he sat me down and told me that it was just lust. Sure felt like love to me. It's amazing what GOOD dick will do to a woman. (Just ask Whitney Houston)

I am always asked, "what do I look for in a man?" What I am most attracted, more than a man's physical appearance is his personality. I need a very strong, very dominate man. I know it may seem like I contradict myself a lot but I like what I like. I want a man that can take charge. I want a real man that will not let me walk over him. That being said, that doesn't mean I want an abusive man either. I have been there and done that. Trust and believe, the next man that raises a hand to me will be featured as the victim on an episode of SNAPPED. I ain't playing that shit again.

Lust to Love?

I had envisioned a hundred times

in my mind

what it would feel like to make love to you,

it was strange to me because I didn't really

even know you

but your voice had this affect on me; already,

your words softly caressing my body

and from the first moment I laid eyes on you,

I knew,

I could feel this undeniable chemistry. See

you are beautiful to me

Like chocolate silk with a graceful groove,

you're liquid smooth,

I am completely lost in the essence of you

You have become my object of desire, fueling

the fire of passion and heat

Your gifted tongue keeps finding that spot

where my thighs meet

And you licked so lavishly the liquid of my

love

that even though your size intimidated me

I wanted to feel it sliding into me

but I was shocked by the sheer wetness of my

pussy

and how it stretched to accommodate your

massive masculinity

See you made love to my mind first

making me have a thirst

for you that only your love making could

satisfy

so that is why

I welcomed you into me, with cries of ecstasy.

You have done something to me that no man or

woman could do

You made me submit to you

My body no longer belonged to me, it belonged
to you
to do completely what you want to
And oh the things you did to it
I must admit, some of the acts committed I
wanted to tell you to quit
but I have never felt anything like it before
and I went from wanting you to stop to wanting
some more.
It is strange to feel the worst pain and best
pleasure at the same time
pain so intense it made me climb
away as if I was under attack
but pleasure so intense it made me grind my
pussy back
then giving the head a few licks to taste my
own cum on the tip of your dick
making my cries go from no, don't, please
stop,
to please don't stop and climbing on top

of you to ride and feel that pussy glide

up and down with each stroke until my pussy

was soaking wet

yet even when I was sore, I still wanted more

and you flipped me over putting me on all

fours

and tore up what was rightfully yours

fucking me till I couldn't take no more

Why did you have to keep your face buried deep

in my moisture?

You have become my new obsession, my love

lesson, my sweet torture.

You have left me so shaken and confused I

wasn't expecting this

See I was supposed to make you fall in love

with that first kiss

instead I am lost in your abyss of passion

wishing I could dismiss what's happening,

the nagging persistence in my heart.

Sex is not love; love is not lust I know all
this is true
But damn, I have fallen for you, so now what
do I do?

Daddy's Girl

(Whispered nice and slow to your man)

Sit down right there in your chair and relax

I've ran your bath water and when you're ready

I'll be in to wash your back

When you're done bathing, I'll get the towel and dry you

Then lay down on the bed so I can rub hot oil on you too

Do you like that daddy?

Do I make you smile?

Relax Daddy

Let me cater to you for a while

I'm going to give you something that you can feel

You stand up daddy and make me kneel

I want to make your whole body jerk and shake with convulsions

I want to feel you on my tongue feel your explosion

I want to taste you, daddy, swallow you like your seed

Was all the nourishment my body would ever need?

I want you so deep in my throat I can barely breathe

Ummmmmm that's it daddy give every drop to me

I want your sex daddy

Your still erect wow

I can see that you are ready for some real loving now

How do you want it daddy?

You know this pussy is yours

Tell me what you like

Your pleasure is what I'm here for

In front of the mirror daddy?

Oooooo you know I like it like that

With my ass in the air and my chest pressed down flat

Holding me

Spank my Ass

Controlling me

Make me submit

ohhhh Reach under me and rub that clit

Ohhhhh Shit daddy

You've got my pussy so wet

I've came twice but I'm not done yet

Turn over daddy and let me ride

Till I can feel you cumming inside

Hold me tight daddy, squeeze my thighs

And while you're cumming look deep in my eyes

Did I make you happy daddy, did I satisfy you?

I'll let you sleep for a minute, but don't think I'm through

Rest for now Daddy because when you wake

I'm inviting my girlfriend over for our next play date.

My chocolate man

You are my chocolate man; your color is polished smooth like exquisite ebony; A deep, rich mocha like the color of fine mahogany, you are beautiful to me

Incredibly sexy and when we make love it is sweeter than anything made by Hershey

I have a fetish for you now, an addiction that only your love making can cure

You're making me stay on my knees worshipping you like you were my savior

You got me wanting to be with you every day, every second of every day, every single minute

I had never had a man make me cry, bring me to tears from eating my pussy, but you did it

And now I'm gone, fantasizing about you when I'm at home, in my bed alone, moaning and groaning, longing for you, clenching the sheets hoping for the slightest whiff of your cologne

Reminiscing about riding your face in a 69 and at times you would spank my ass while I was on top

And then you were drinking my cum like it was Maxwell House umm ummmm good to the last drop, let me stop before I am on the phone calling you back over when you just left a minute ago

We have fucked every day this week but you still got me wanting some more

and I am trying to gratify myself by masturbating

but it's like eating ice when I'm starving, it does nothing for this craving, it can't satisfy this hunger I have for the that thing. Damn this was just supposed to be a fling, but

I want you, I don't understand

How did it go from being a one night stand to me wanting you to be my man? Dammit you got me twisted, all over some good dick, I am soooo not used to this

Got me wanting to give you other bitches just to see if you give them the same kind of bliss

Crazy right? I know this is but it's like every time you walk through the door

 my knees automatically hit the floor

My mouth craves you, your taste, your texture, your feel against my tongue

And when it comes to making love I am an experienced woman

 but your dick is so big that it makes me feel like a virgin all over again.

You should have warned me before stepping into the lion's den that after fucking with you my pussy would

need a day or two to mend

I'm going to have to go out and find a

girlfriend just so that she can help me keep

up with you

wait now that I'm thinking about it a

girlfriend might not help so I better go get

two.

The Musician and the Poet

True love making requires the use of all 5 of
your senses: sight, smell, and touch, taste
and sound too

Sex is just sex making love is sublime and
true love making will excite you, renew you,
cause a sexual rebirth in you

All love making begins with sight; you are
such a visual creature, your desire starts by
what you see

So I am naked with high heels and boy shorts
that only cover the top of my booty

You see cause even though I am not a size two
you love the way I move

and I allow you to marvel in the beauty of my
softness and the curves of my body

and you like that I seductively, strategically
place mirrors all around the room

and I have slow jams playing but the sweetest
music comes from making love
so let me turn down this volume.
The room is already lightly scented from the
candles of jasmine that I have been burning
but the smell of another human can be
intoxicating, causing a lustful yearning
God intended for us to enjoy the scent of one
another so a women's pheromones are a cue
To let her partner know she is ready to be
made love to that she wants and needs to be
taken by you
So breathe me in baby, can you smell my desire
for you?
Now touch me baby, I want to savor every touch
of your finger, kiss of your lips
Feel of your breath against the back of my
neck while you grabbing my hips
Ummmm I am loving this

but I am making love to YOUR senses so our
roles are switched

so I begin to kiss your chest, your neck

tonguing a trail to your ears

I don't want you to just hear

I want you to feel my breathy whispers, moans

and groans in your ear

 Voulez-Vous Coucher Avec Moi? I want to put
you to bed

 Patti and J Holiday lyrics being mixed in my
head

Damn I'm supposed to be turning you on but you

got me wanting you instead

You are just so sexy; this is torturing me so

I get down on my knees

And beg you to please, please feed this

hunger, quench my thirst, and satisfy this
need

Calm this overwhelming craving I have to taste

your seed

And holding firmly to the back of my head you

shutter and release

and your taste is sweeter than honey to me

but I'm not getting away that easily

and you spread my legs putting your velvet

soft tongue on my pussy

and I can hardly take it and I go from pulling

the dreads on your head

to clenching a fistful of the bedspread

to grinding my pussy against your lips, the

lips only musicians had

from trying to cum to cumming and then trying

to run

trying to get away from your skilled tongue

ohhhhh to be so gifted and so young

you putting me in my favorite position, taking

me to the limit

I need to feel you inside me, stroking me

deeply

the combining of all of our senses united in

perfect harmony

watching you in the mirror hitting it from the

back, the smell of shea butter and your

favorite cologne DJ's Black

Your taste is still lingering on my tongue

I feel your dick throbbing you are about to

cum, my pussy wrapping around you

squeezing you, pleasing you

the sound of flesh against flesh, me

confessing this is the best sex

and you professing that this is your pussy and

I agree

and you see though I've always loved chocolate

this butterscotch brother is hitting it Right!

Leaving me drained my faced flushed scarlet

loving me like you love that trumpet,

the musician and the poet unite

Your Favorite Chair

I really should just throw your favorite chair
out so I can get you off my mind
Cause I am sitting here staring at it again
for the hundredth time
Reminiscing about how u would sit down in that
chair after a hard day's work to unwind.
You never made it further than that chair,
sitting down while I kneeled to take off your
boots
And you only getting back up long enough to
shower and eat the dinner that I prepared for
you.
Then back to your favorite chair. I miss those
days
It seems like that piece of furniture was just
made for sex
So many memories held in an inanimate object

Like all the head I gave u while you were
sitting in that very spot
And how it would get so good to you that you
would try to make me stop
But I would not, not until I had swallowed
every single drop
I miss those days
And the way we used to use your chair when we
role played
How you were my saddle and I would straddle
you and ride u into the sunset
And how I would be your little girl and you
would tell me to cum sit on daddy's lap
And how u would pretend to be my boss and fire
me
And how I would try to convince you not to by
dropping to my knees
And showing you I don't need any type of
degrees to get the job done
 And to make sure you were pleased

And I always got to keep my job

and I remember the times when you were a cop

And would handle me all rough

Pushing me over the back of your chair and

putting on the cuffs

And you telling me that if I do as u say I can

avoid jail time

And with my hands still in cuff, you take me

from behind

I miss those days

and we haven't been together now for a minute

So I need to either get rid of your favorite

chair or find someone new to sit in it

Any Volunteers?

Chapter 9

My life as a

POEM

I've had a few years now to adjust to the many life changes that I've been through. It was a big adjustment for me to go back to being single. Being single again as I was about to enter my forties was probably scarier for me than the whole coming out process. I never really had much of an opportunity to date before I got married and over the years, dating has changed. A good majority of people nowadays meet on the internet. The concept is great but the reality can be scary. You are talking to a stranger that could pretend to be anybody that they want to be. When you meet that person in real life a lot of times the internet personality doesn't match up with what you get in the real world. There are dating sites for lesbians such as Downelink and Pinkcupid that are geared specifically for hooking up women. I have found more success on finding single, available females on regular sites such as Facebook and Tagged. I spoke earlier about being in a relationship with a closeted girl whose uncle and father are both ministers. She is a very beautiful girl and I met her on Tagged. Her entire family is very much involved in the church. So she was in the closet, like in the back of the closet, under a pile of dirty clothes, where the cobwebs were. She explained that in her family the fact that she had children out of wedlock was more acceptable than her bisexuality. She was living a lie. Not only living a lie but she was a hypocrite. She would stand up in church and condemn homosexuality while knowing in her heart that she was a member of the same population she was condemning. I was not surprised by the allegations that surfaced concerning prominent church leaders like Bishop Eddie Long. Homosexuality is rampant in the church. I am still amazed at how many people will stand up in church and condemn homosexuality before going home to their gay lovers. The girl I met was no different. She would declare boldly and proudly that homosexuality was an abomination. She would condemn all gay people to hell. But she loved women. After our first date we didn't immediately begin a relationship even though I was very attracted to her. Once I had come out to my family, I had no intentions of going back in. I didn't know if I could date someone that was not open about their sexuality. I was dragged out the closet kicking and screaming, but once I was out, I refused to go back in. Dating someone that was still in meant I would have to go back to sneaking, hiding, and lying. But did I tell you that this girl was beautiful? No matter how much I didn't want to date her, I kept thinking about her. And that is when I finally sent her a text message of me kissing a girl and asking her if she wanted to be next. She immediately responded back and asked, "Can I be next?" HELL YES!!! And with that we began a secretive two-year relationship.

I have to admit coming out the closet definitely enhanced my love life. See, once I was able to stand up in a public forum and announce that I was bisexual and proud of it; it upped my stock in the dating world. Men hit on me because they thought that if they got with me it would increase their odds of having a threesome. Straight women (especially the married kind) hit on me because they didn't have to worry about accidently coming on to another straight woman and being rejected. They knew what I was. Bisexual women that were both in the closet and out of the closet hit on me. And of course, lesbians hit on me as well. There is a saying that goes homosexuality is just as limiting as heterosexuality. People should be allowed to love whoever they choose to love regardless of gender. After many years of fighting this moral battle within myself I have finally come to accept my love of people. Sex is secondary. I fall in love with the person. Sometimes that person is a guy and sometimes that person is a girl. Love knows no limits and has no boundaries. I am comfortable in the skin that I am in and I look forward to what life has in store. I have become a very brutally honest person. I don't pull punches and very rarely, if ever, do I bite my tongue. I have taken the good and the bad and molded it together to make… me. And nobody can love me more than I love myself. When I came to this point in life it helped me to become patient in my search for love. I am not in a hurry anymore. When it happens, it happens and I will be ready. I am looking for quality not quantity. Until that happens I will continue to enjoy this journey of self discovery. I will continue to be happy being ME!

I AM NOT A SIZE 2

I am not a size 2 and I will never be, but I
know to be sexy is more than the size of your
dress beauty comes in all sizes, yes, even in
a 20.

See I started out thin and as my waist began
to expand I noticed that I was becoming more
in demand. The attention my curves commanded
reminds me of the voluptuous women in the
grand paintings by Ruben.

So it is no surprise when men look at me that
they can't disguise what arises when their
eyes see the abundance of soft flesh in my
belly, my ass, my thighs, and skinny girls
despise me because they I understand why men
love me, but I mind, I love their envy. It
motivates me.

See I have figured out what they have not. It
I matter what type of body I got. The sexiest

asset on a woman is her confidence and attitude. It is sexy when you are not ashamed to be nude when you care more about yourself and not how you are viewed.

I am not ashamed to be myself, honest to a fault, and forward as hell. I am unbiased, make no apologies and I refuse to live my life in a shell. When the truth was revealed, I was flirted with because I didn't hold my weight up as a shield. I was unyielding in my love of self. Not conceited, just self aware.

Thin beauty is a modern day phenomenon once upon a time, a penchant for plump women was not a crime or anything to be embarrassed about, and having a full-bodied woman in Africa was considered a symbol of clout.

Oh and the sex, the sex.

I have heard men talk about fat women and how they would never do a big girl, I tell them you have no idea what you are missing a big girl will rock your world

so to all you men out there here is my warning

we will have you calling your mama at 4 in the

morning

leave you curled up in a fetal position

sucking your thumb

Have you chasing us, wondering if there is

more to come

See big girls I cry, we take all of it, we

won't break so be rough we can handle that

shit and I think because we are fat we are not

fit, so please I come at us with a 30 second

hit and you know we love to eat

so we swallow, not spit

And the sexiest vision that you will ever find

is the sway in our spine

and the ripples our ass makes when you hit us

from behind

like the waves in the ocean

and that is why we have the devotion of men
that love to make love to and can't let go
because they are so into us.

See, I am not a size 2 and I will never be,
but I know to be sexy is more than the size of
your dress beauty comes in all sizes, yes,
even in a 20.

A letter to haters, future, present and past

Dear Haters Future, present and past

Backstabbers are quite pleasant and supportive

on the surface but that's just a mask

You know from kids to adults ain't a damn

thing changed,

my haters have always been the same,

they still hating on the player instead of

hating on the game,

I hope you choke every time you spit on my

name

And even though you're lacking intact, I have

always tried to be nonviolent, that's a fact

But I ought to stab you in the throat with the

knife you left in my back.

Yellow streaks down their back, got all these

haters shaking in fear

quick to talk shit when I'm not around but scared to do it when I'm near

Because in dealing with backstabbers one thing you will learn

They will smile in your face, then talk about you the minute your back is turned

In the words of Marilyn Monroe

"If you are gonna be two-faced at least make sure one of your faces is pretty".

I know many will agree, some can ACT like friends so well they should win an award from the Academy,

I'm trying to teach you all a lesson so forgive me if I seem to rant

But if you have doubts about whether you can trust someone…chances are you can't

It is easy to have friends when you are up, doing well, fancy house, and nice car

But when you are down is when you find out who your real friends are

Behind ever successful person is a pack of
haters, so just take their hating as flattery
 And try to understand that hating goes hand
in hand with ignorance and jealousy
But I just sing Que Sera Sera, whatever will
be will be
cause your really hate yourself, that is why
you hating on me.
You see, even Jesus had haters and he didn't
do anything to make enemies
Temple guards, Scribes, Satan, Judas and even
the Chief Priest,
so If they hated on Jesus, I can't expect the
whole world to love me
Cause those that loved Jesus in the beginning
would end up being the same ones that
condemned him
See, I never cared about making friends so I
can care less about losing them

"All the mistakes in the world couldn't measure up to the day I thought I could trust you."

So do me a favor, while you're stabbing my back, can you kiss my ass too.

P. S. If you are a hater and jealousy makes you THINK you can write a poem about me; just remember I could eat alphabet soup and shit out better poetry

Sincerely, Me

An apology to my sons

I owe all my sons an apology. I need to tell

each of you that I am sorry

That while you were studying math, English and

biology

I should have been teaching you history, our

history,

as Black women there is no mystery

as to what we went through but I should have

made you see how our past affects you.

Our history was not the picture perfect

passages written in textbooks

Look from our mother's arms they took

us and we wonder why each generation gets

worse

with the perverse

 love for a people that have brutalized us

enslaving our minds to believe that a black

woman is a curse.

Whipped and stripped

Black women and white men had an open sexual
relationship

Not only was the Black woman brought down,

but she was now dirty, used, abused, and
passed around

and Black men could not deal with that back
then

And it still affects them today

The way we were treated as a Black female

devastated the Black Male

ego which was already frail

On the other side, the white woman was held up
as being pure

and the White man would kill to ensure, that

his ideal example of womanhood was secure.

She was completely off limits to the black man

and if his eyes were to land

on a white woman it meant death at his
master's hand

by whipping, hanging, and castration, burning,

drowning and decapitation.

So what is the attraction? I will explain it

like this

Left alone, the opposing sides of a rubber

band are not drawn to one another,

but pull them apart and the slightest give

sends the two ends rushing toward each other.

It was the ability to have something that was

out of reach

and this is why I owe you an apology because I

failed to teach.

I should have taught you the story of Yusuf

Hawkins and Emmitt Till and how for looking at

a white woman he was killed.

Your freedom to love whomever you choose came

at a hefty price

You owe this right to many strong Black women

that paid the cost with their life

I cringe every time I hear one of you say you don't date your own.

And you start listing the problems of Black women and what you think is wrong

How can you not love the look of a woman that looks like your mother?

Who looks like the women that died for your freedom to simply love one another

I should have taught you the difference between dating preference and dating prejudice.

I should have made you see that to love them doesn't mean you have to hate me.

I should have taught you about the dire consequences that come from self loathing

About the lie of white beauty that the mass media promoted

Using hair straighteners, color contacts and skin lighteners, to try to erase, every little trace

Of the black that made our people beautiful,

that makes us a strong, proud race

I am sorry dear sons, please forgive me, is my

impassioned plea that I never taught you in

order to love them doesn't mean you have to

hate me

Boys to Men

I have worked myself quite literally, to death
and sometimes my sons won't even say thank you
like it's a waste of their breath
ok son, so now you think you're too old to
listen to what your mama has to say
Reminding me that you are grown just because
you've passed your 18th birthday
You want to be a man? Stop blaming and
resenting your parents, we didn't have to have
you we could have waited
But we put our dreams on hold to keep you fed,
clothed, entertained, healthy and educated
Do you think that it is your birthright? Just
because you have testicle you were born to be
a man
 Boy please, you got a lot to learn, so let me
help you understand

My father was a man, started picking cotton in

the fields at the age of five

On the same plantation that owned his

grandparents, where his parents were

sharecroppers until they died

And no that doesn't make him a man, but it

helped him understand the value of hard work.

The school he went to was 10 miles down the

road and I know that doesn't seem like a lot

But it is when you don't have a car or a bus

and the only transportation you've got

are your own two feet

10 miles is a lot

And every day without missing a beat

he would pack his lunch of beans and

cornbread and make his way

But his family needed him to work so even

though he wanted to stay

he had to quit school in the 9th grade

And no that doesn't make him a man, but it made him understand the importance of education

When he had become an adult he met my mom, a widowed mother of five

But he didn't care

that she had five kids he still made her his wife and he devoted his life

to not only raising her five kids that were already there but also the 7 more that they shared

He never made a difference in any of us because even if he wasn't the biological we were all his

When people asked, I never heard him once say I have 7 children, but rather I have 12 kids

And no that doesn't make him a man, but it made him understand the importance of family

My father knew that hard work, education, and
family were just the building blocks of a
strong foundation
And being a man was a title you earn by the
daily application of honesty
good will, faith, love, hope, accountability,
self-confidence, self-knowledge and integrity
So you think you are a man, Boy please

All my single ladies

Why do people talk about being single like it
is some damn disease?
Like it's contagious and you might catch it if
you stand too close to me, please
I hear all the time, so why are you still
single? What's wrong with you?
Nothing, I just refuse
to live in a world of bullshit and come home
and take more bullshit from you.
Now don't get me wrong, I'm not knocking
marriage
cause for 20 years I did
the whole being a wife and having kids
and there is nothing wrong with that
but 70 % of single women are black
42 % will never marry and that is a fact
Society makes us feel like there is nothing
worse

and that being a single Black woman is some
kind of curse

Well that was simply how things were done back
then

So instead of looking at Black women

Find out what the hell is wrong with Black Men

Ya'll love our sex and are quick to get on it

But you still slow to put a ring on it

We were good enough to get you a seat on the
front of the bus

But not good enough for you to marry us

I was good enough to help you be free but not
good enough for you to marry me

Good enough to be the mother of your child
but not good enough for you to take down the
aisle

good enough for you to make love to

but not good enough for you to say I do

Good enough for you to shack up with for life

But not good enough for you to make your wife

Good enough to deal with all your faults and bullshit

but not good enough to get you to commit

We are good enough to be your woman, lover and friend,

But not good enough to be your legal next of kin

Single, Black, Beautiful Queens, don't fall victim to those fairytale dreams

And don't think that you are less than a woman because you don't have a man

Being single can be a blessing not a curse, do you understand

Don't hold onto that loser cause you think a piece of man is better than none

Cause if you do your relationship was doomed before it had even begun

Chapter 10

Miscellaneous Poems

Time Machine

Reminiscing about the remember when...

and I'm thinking about the way back then...

Saying to myself I wish I could go back again

Back to days of innocence

Like back when having fun was more important

than the win

Back when you could put all your trust in your

next of kin

back before you learned that sometimes a

simple grin is used to mask the evil within

Back when the only CHANCE you took was in a

Monopoly game

Instead of hustling in the streets, waiting on

your 15 minutes of fame

Like when tomorrow's newspaper headline reads,

Dope Dealer found slain

Back when all little girls dreamed

about being the homecoming queen?

But because of YOU and how you chose to make

your green

little girls are becoming crack fiends

selling their bodies by the time they are

thirteen

And you don't even care that you contribute to

these things

It's all just a means to an end right?

 as long as it's not your sister, your

daughter, your wife

You didn't create crack so making money off

addiction is a perk

And you're so generous that you gave your

little brother work

You're proud of your little brother, the trap

star

Rolling around in a Benz, till someone jacked

him for that car

now the block is talking about who killed your

brother J. R.

So here we are…

Reminiscing about the remember when…

and I'm thinking about the way back then…

Saying to myself, I wish I could go back again

Back to days of innocence

Like back when the most important event in

your life was Saturday morning cartoons

Back when you could tune out the world and

just lie in bed eating peanut butter with a

spoon

Back when you could just sit in the tub until

you looked like a prune

That was until your Uncle Joe came into the

bathroom

And even though back then he had always called

you his baby

He did things to you he should have only done

to his old lady

Took your virginity without regret, left you

in a puddle of your own blood, yet

He blamed you, said you would be in trouble if you didn't keep his secret

Even though you tried to block it out you just couldn't forget

That day in the bathroom when your Uncle Joe stole your innocence

Now you can't go back to being a child because everything has changed

You didn't feel like the other kids growing up, naw, you just weren't the same

So at 16 years old you put a gun to Uncle Joe's head and blew out his brains

and everybody wonders what happened, but it's too late now for them to start asking

so we are left...

Reminiscing about the remember when...

and I'm thinking about the way back then...

Saying to myself I wish I could go back again

Back to days of innocence

Back when a relationship was started by the passing of a note

I like you ...do you like me? check yes or no; is all he wrote

And when you walked to school your books he would tote

And even though you didn't want to gloat, if they had a best boyfriend in the world contest he would definitely get your vote

And of course like the song goes, first comes love then comes marriage

And 6 months after the wedding, here you come with a baby carriage

6 months later is when the beating first start,

Even though you knew you needed to leave you couldn't stand being apart

How could you leave this man that had been your heart?

So after 5 years and 2 babies, he decides to

he wants to start seeing other ladies

He blamed you, saying your body just didn't

look the same

You weren't sexy or fine to him anymore after

the babies came

But his side chic Elaine, has the big disease

with the little name

Now here we go again...

Reminiscing about the remember when...

and I'm thinking about the way back then...

Saying to myself I wish I could go back again

Back to days of innocence

Fantasy Island

Fantasies are just that, FANTASIES, it's just
sexually mind play
And just because you have a fantasy doesn't
mean you will make it reality
I am a women and I fantasize about sex just
like men do
Sometimes I wish I could make some of those
fantasies come true
So I am about to share some top female
fantasies with you
Because most men, especially the married ones
don't have a clue
That their women probably have the same
fantasies too
Fantasy #1 she wants to dominate you, like you
see the Mistresses on TV does

With you down on your knees, dog collar on
kissing her boot

Dressed all in leather, boot on your back,
whip in hand

you will do what the fuck Mistress S tells u
to do, understand

Fantasy # 2 involves the man being the
dominate mate

We want a powerful man to hold us in an
embrace

Woman fantasizes about you pinning her down,
thrusting her thighs apart with your knees

And without even a kiss you taking her
savagely

She fantasizes about you fucking her as rough
and as hard as you can

Fuck that metrosexual love making bullshit; we
want to be fucked by a REAL MAN

Next fantasy, some of ya'll will not want to
admit, but stop acting prudent

Cause men are not the only one with the
fantasy about the teacher and the student
Women love the idea of dressing up like a
naughty school girl as often as they can
 Loads of grown ass women fantasize about
getting a proper spanking from their man.
Most women will never act out the next fantasy
due to the danger
Since this fantasy involves sex with a
complete stranger
The threesome with another woman should not be
a surprise,
Most women have this unexplored lesbian side
Unlike men who can't look at another man
sexually without disgust
Women notice other women's hair, clothes,
shape, breast and butt
The next fantasy involves the woman being
worshiped by two gorgeous men

It could be as simple as getting fucked while giving head, or double penetration

For most women this fantasy is the ultimate taboo, so it will stay just her imagination

If you think women don't enjoy watching other people get it on, you're completely mistaken.

She acts like she is watching a flick for you and it doesn't affect her…She Faking

And the last fantasy is the desire a woman has to be watched by others

Initially she may say no to a homemade flick but after the first one she'll want to make another

Or they take the fantasies even further than flicks and pictures in some case

And will daydream about you fucking her in a very public place

Men I just wanted to give you a few suggestions to do

Whenever you think about making your woman's
fantasies come true

So talk to each other and find out what the
other one likes

And maybe you can make each other's fantasies
come true tonight

Freedom Pleas?

My ancestors overcame 300 years of bondage so that I could have a voice,

Yet I suffer in silence

They were tortured, beaten and killed so that one day I would have a choice

And I choose to stay

How would my ancestors feel about me today, knowing the way, that I allow you to continually abuse me?

Since slavery ended I don't have abolitionist or underground railroads to help me be free

I was never taught how to follow the north star when I flee

I don't have a Fiddler like Kunta to save me from your wrath when you are angry

There is no Cinque with "Give us, us free" pleas for sympathy

Just a hand thrown up in a feeble attempt to shield my face from your brutality

There will be no soldiers dressed in blue coming to liberate me; I don't get a Civil war

No Emancipation Proclamation saying I am ME, and not your property anymore

So I endure

And I try to hide the black eyes, and disguise the bruises with make up

and I pray to God that one day before it's too late you will wake up

and realize that love is patient and love is kind, that love is not rude

love is not easily angered; love does not
delight in evil but rejoices in truth

and you will love me the way that my God loves
you, unconditionally

Why do I make you so angry, why do you hate me
so much

You never dealt with your abusive past so you
use alcohol as your crutch

And make me endure the brunt of your anger and
rage

Making me a slave bound by love's shackles,
treating me worse than an animal caged

Eventually an abused dog will turn on its
master, and it's not being a traitor

Like Sophia said in the color purple, Bash
Mister's head in and worry about heaven later

But like my ancestors who demanded to be free
from their oppressor's tyranny,

I'm not going to wait on you to get an epiphany, I am going to demand, by any means necessary, and end to your cruelty

If you don't comply, I am going to have to choose between loving you and loving me

And on that day, I will be like Nat Turner and the rebel slaves, so be cautious when you sleep

I have stopped blaming me for your faults, I once was lost but now I'm found

And I will never ever again allow the hand that I hold to hold me do

Deadbeat

How dare you complain about paying child
support
All up and arms because you were ordered to
pay $250 by family court
Acting such a fool that they had to escort you
out of the courtroom and transport your ass to
jail
And now anyone that will listen, you want to
tell them your child support tale
Fuck You!
Here is what we will do, come get your kids
and keep your little two hundred and fifty
dollars
Buy diapers for your daughter and take your
son every two weeks to visit the barber
And don't get any sleep at night cause you
baby girl woke up hollering

Or take them school shopping and try to buy them Jordan's on Converse money

And try buying food to feed two kids with no assistance from the county

how far do you think that $250 will go when you have two kids that are hungry?

Try putting a roof over your kid's head

You can keep your $250 as long as you are willing to pay for them a home with lights and gas

Keep all your money just provide them with utilities…water, phone, and cable instead

Keep that $250 and pay for their insurances… medical, dental, and life.

I shouldn't complain about working two jobs and giving my money to babysitters, right?

I mean none of this should cause me any strife

You don't want to pay child support for our two kids but you got another on the way with your wife

That is why, I just keep on doing what I need
to do to take care of OUR kids
And you keep on being the bitch you are and
whining about what the child support folks did
Put you in jail
Took your driver's license away
I wish you would try being a full time parent
for just one day
I am getting tired of how you treat our kids,
I don't know how much more I can take
You call you baby girl an accident and your
oldest son a mistake
And it breaks my heart when they cry because
they miss you
Those are times I think about you missing boo
Or better than that, I think all dead beat
dads should be chemically castrated
So they can no longer produce children that
they will resent or later end up hating

Cause the way you treat OUR kids make me want to do something to you

Since you baby your car more than your kids, I want to flatten all 4 tires and put sugar in your tank too

But I have to just have faith and keep believing

Cause I know 2 wrongs don't make a right but it damn sure makes it even

Dictionary

LESBIAN 101 - DEFINITIONS

Baby Dyke

Definition: A young lesbian or someone who is just coming out of the closet also called a dyke in training

Bi-Curious

Definition: To be bi-curious is to be questioning your sexual orientation. You're not sure if you are bisexual, but you have a curiosity about it. You're openly questioning if you are bisexual or not.

Bisexual

Definition: A person who is sexually and emotionally attracted to both women and men.

Bulldagger

Definition: This is a term that was used in the 1920s to define a very butch lesbian. Often African American.

Butch

Definition: A woman who adopts what would be considered masculine characteristics.

Ex-Gay Reparative Therapy

Definition: Ex-gay reparative therapy attempts to change a person's sexual orientation from gay, lesbian or bisexual to straight. The ex-gay movement is faith-based and believes people can willfully change their sexual orientation through counseling and prayer.

Dyke

Definition: Another word for lesbian. Usually is only used by people who are gay, lesbian, bisexual or trans. A straight person using this word may offend some people.

Femme

Definition: A feminine lesbian.

Also Known As: lipstick lesbian

Definition: The ability to determine who is and isn't gay is called gaydar.

Lesbian

Definition: A woman who is sexually and emotionally attracted to other women.

Also Known As: dyke, homosexual woman

Definition: Used as an abbreviation for Lesbian, Gay, Bisexual and Trans.

Out of the Closet

Definition: Being open about one's sexual orientation.

Pansexual

Definition: A pansexual is someone who is attracted people of many genders.

Sexual Orientation

Definition: Who you are attracted to can be gay, straight, lesbian or bisexual.

Stud Lesbian

Definition: A dominant lesbian, usually butch, often African American.

Transsexual

Definition: A person with the urge to be the opposite sex. They may or may not choose to have gender reassignment surgery.

Transgender

Definition: A person whose gender expression is different from how society says they are "supposed" to be. Transgender can be an umbrella term for cross-dressers, transsexuals, intersex people and other gender-variant individuals. Transgender people may or may not decide to take hormones or have sex-reassignment surgery.

About the Author

Adisa Salim was born in Chicago, Il. She currently lives in Alabama. She is a spoken word artist and motivational speaker. Adisa the owner and creative force behind the Queen Adisa brand.

www.queenadisa.com